Fight Naked

Taking your marriage from
Surviving to Thriving

By Mark and Karen Stevens

Introduction

Couples ask us all the time, "what is the secret to your 45+ years of marriage" and we jokingly answer, "Fight Naked and Sleep Naked!" This has been our standard go-to answer to couples and we are known as the "Fight Naked" couple. One of our other secrets is, to be best friends. We started out as best friends and we have maintained that friendship above all others for 50 years!

It is true, that when you get into an argument, it's hard to keep the fight going and stay angry ifyou take your clothes off, at least from a man's perspective!

We run a ministry called the www.marriage Refuge.com where we see couples move from "Surviving to Thriving" in their marriage. As ordained pastors we have seen the need for restoring marriages. We offer a place of refuge for couples to go to really understand the challenges facing their marriage. We use an analysis tool called "The Couple Check-up" that quickly points out their marriage challenges. Our goal is to make adjustments that can get your marriage backon track.

We have found through "The Couple Check-up" we can pinpoint a couple's areas of strength and areas for growth. We focus on the areas for growth and develop an action plan with accountability.

This book is designed as a workbook to help you take the next steps in giving you tools to help you move your marriage from *surviving to thriving*. Who knows, maybe you will start "fighting naked and sleeping naked" like we do!

Mark and Karen Stevens

Contents

How to Use this "Work" Book

This workbook is designed to help you take steps towards improving your marriage. The "work" in the **work**book is important to focus on since marriage is "Work!" We have found there are no shortcuts, or a pill you can take to improve your marriage, it takes "work" from both of you. Over the years we have met with hundreds of couples and found that most of them want to talk about their challenges, and then have us fix them! We have found that the only way to improve your marriage is for the couple to act and change their individual behavior! No one can change another person; the change comes from us individually.

The definition of insanity is "doing the same things over and over and expecting different results!" We want to give you practical applications that you can start doing today to break the insanity cycle.

You can use this workbook with "The Couple Check-up" report that you may have taken, or you can do your own analysis of the areas you need to grow in. We find that most couples know what their main growth areas are and can follow this guide.

Easy steps to follow:

1. List your areas of strengths and areas for growth
2. Circle your top growth areas
3. Find the corresponding workbook pages
4. Set goals at the end of each chapter
5. Set action steps.

One of the best ways to hold yourself accountable is to share your goals publicly. Let your friends or family know how you are improving your marriage by taking action and sharing them. We are collecting the action steps and goals on our Facebook page @theMarriageRefuge. You can also contact us at the www.marriageRefuge.com and tell us how you are doing.

We pray that God will move you to go from *Surviving* in your marriage to *Thriving!*

Your Current Condition

We have found that most couples know their top strengths areas and their top growth areas. If you completed "The Couple Check-up" report you can refer to that report, otherwise you can fill in the blanks below based on your intuition.

List your top Strength Areas

List your top Growth Areas

Top 4 Growth Areas

Circle the top 4 Growth Areas in your Marriage

Communications - Pages 5-11
Conflict Resolution – Pages 12-18
Financial Management – Pages 19-24
Leisure Activities – Pages 25-32
Sexual Relations – Pages 33-37
Roles and Responsibility – Pages 38-42
Spiritual Beliefs – Pages 43-48

After Circling the top four go to each page for each section

Communications

Communications is the #1 challenge we've seen over the past 30 years with almost all couples. When there is poor communication, it effects all aspects of your marriage.

Understand this, my dear brothers and sisters: You must all be quick to listen, slow to speak, and slow to get angry. — James 1:19

Communications

Start with LISTENING!

Proper Listening Habits

Focus on

- What is being said the Way it is being said, tone and body language.
- Clarification of valid points Ask Questions for Understanding.

Rather than

- How you feel about what is said
- The Words only Defense of incorrect Accusations Indictments Judgement

Communications

Assertive and Active Listening

Assertiveness is the ability to express your feelings and ask for what you want in your relationship.

Active Listening is the ability to let your partner know you understand them by restating their message.

In sharing your Wish List with your partner, you are demonstrating your Assertive skills. In gving feedback to your partner about their Wish List, you will be demonstrating your Active Listening Skills.

Make a Wish List of three things you would like more or less of in your relationship

1. _____

2._____

3._____

Communications

We All Use Three Forms of Communications

100% of Communication is made up in these three areas. Write in your best guess, the percentages that equal 100%*

1. **Content** – written word (guess)_____% (answer)_____%

2. **Body Language** – your bodies physical movement (guess)_____% (answer)_____%

3. **Voice & Tone** – sound and pitch of voice (guess)_____% (answer)___%

How does this apply to your communications with your partner?

Dr. Albert Mehrabian's 7-38-55 Communications Model

Answers
Content 7%
Body Language 55%
Voice & Tone 38%

Communication – What Does God's Word Say

Ephesians 4:14, 29

Proverbs 10:19

Proverbs 12:18

Proverbs 15:1, 28

Proverbs 18:2, 13, 21

Proverbs 29:20

I Peter 3:7

Colossians 3:8

Colossians 4:6

Psalms 19:14 Psalms

141:3 Matthew 12:36

James 1:26

Communication Goals

- Examples of Goals:
  - Face to Face communications (no electronics or kids) once a day for 15 minutes. Share your day or experiences.
  - Date night once a week.
  - Make a wish list of things you would like more of or less of in your relationship
  - Ask you spouse to share one positive and one negative from the day.
  - Pray over communications

Goals

_____ completion date _

_____ completion date _

_____ completion date _

Conflict Resolution

Conflict resolution follows communication as a big challenge we see in marriages. Most of conflicts we see stem out of poor communications.

Make allowance for each other's faults, and forgive anyone who offends you. Remember, the Lord forgave you, so you must forgive others. – Colossians 3:13

Conflict Resolution

How do you handle Conflict?

Circle the one that best describes your style in conflict

- ! **Fight to Win:** This is the "I win you,lose" or "I'm right, you're wrong" position.
- **Withdraw:** You seek to avoid discomfort at all costs, saying, "I'm uncomfortable, so I'll get out."
- **Yield:** You assume it's far better to go along with the other person's demands than to risk confrontation.

Discuss with your partner:

1. Why are these responses unhealthy in your relationship?

2. Discuss your conflict response with your partner and describe why?

Conflict Resolution

TEN STEPS FOR RESOLVING CONFLICT

All couples have differences and disagreements. Studies show the amount of disagreements are not related to marital happiness as much as how they are handled.

Happy couples do not avoid disagreements; they resolve them while remaining respectful of each other, thereby strengthening their relationship.

This Ten Step Model is a simple, but effective way to resolve conflict while avoiding the common and destructive patterns. Use this model with an ongoing issue in your relationship, as well as future issues.

1. Set a time and and a place for discussion.
2. Define the problem. Be specific:

---

3. List the ways you each contribute to the problem.

---

4. List past attempts to resolve the issue that were not successful.

   _____

   _____

5. Brainstorm 10 possible solutions to the problem. Do not judge or criticize any of the suggestions at this point

   1) _____

   2) _____

   4) _____

   4) _____

   5) _____

   7) _____

   8) _____

   9) _____

   10) _____

6. As objective as possible. Talk about how useful and appropriate each suggestion feels for resolving your issue.

7. Agree on one solution to try: _____

8. Agree *how* you will each work toward this solution. Be as specific as possible.

Partner 1:

_____

Partner 2:

_____

9. Set up another meeting to discuss your progress.

   Place:_____Date:_____

   Time: _____

10. Reward each other for progress. If you notice your partner making a positive contribution toward the solution, praise his/her effort.

Prepare Enrich Workbook for Couples (2014) page 13.

Conflict Resolution and God's Word

I Peter 3:8-11

Ephesians 4:1-6, 26

Romans 12:18

Romans 14:19

Philippians 2:1-3

Colossians 3:13-14

I Corinthians 1:10

2 Corinthians 13:11

Psalms 133:1

Conflict Resolution Goals

- Examples of Goals:
  - Face to Face communications (no electronics or kids) once a day for 15 minutes. Have a stress buffering conversation. Discuss challenges and conflicts
  - Use 10 Steps for Resolving Conflict Form
  - Take a time out

Goals

_____ completion date _

_____ completion date _

_____ completion date _

Financial Management

We see financial conflict in couples that has grown out of a lack of understanding and communications around money.

Yet true godliness with contentment is itself great wealth. After all, we brought nothing with us when we came into the world, and we can't take anything with us when we leave it.

I Timothy 6:6-7

Financial Management

IMPORTANCE OF
FINANCIAL GOALS

Couples argue about finances more than any other topic. Regardless of how much or how little money a couple has, deciding what to purchase and how to spend their money is problematic for most couples.

Typically, most couples focus on only short-term financial goals like: "Today I will pay $100 on my credit card bill." But short-term goals should also take into consideration your long-term goals like:

"We want to save enough to make a down payment on a house." One way to reduce the amount of conflict regarding finances is for you and your partner to discuss and decide on your short-term and long-term financial goals. Setting common goals as a couple can increase your sense of teamwork and collaboration in this complex area of finances.

Identifying and Deciding on Your Financial Goals

Each person should individually brainstorm their short-term and long-term financial goals and then share them with each other. Short-term goals should be what you can achieve in six months to one year. Long term goals might be achieved from one to five years. Remember, your goals should be realistic, clear and specific.

Short-Term Goals (six months to one year)

1. _____
2 _____
3. _____

Long-Term Goals (one to five years)

1. _____
2 _____
3. _____

COUPLE DISCUSSION

- Share your lists with one another.
- What do they have in common? Where are they different?
- Decide together as a couple on your common goals.
- Talk about how you can each contribute to achieving these goals.
- Revisit them from time to time so you stay on track.

Prepare Enrich Workbook for Couples (2014) page 21.

Financial Management God's Way

Luke 16:13

Proverbs 3:9-10

Proverbs 13:11

Ecclesiastes 5:10

Hebrews 13:5

I Timothy 6:6-10

I Timothy 6:17-19

Matthew 6:19-21

Malachi 3:8-10

Financial Management Action Steps

- Examples of Goals:
  - Set a budget
  - Complete a financial course like Dave Ramsey or Crown Ministries
  - Pay-off credit card

Goals

_____ completion date _

_____completion date _

_____ completion date _

Leisure Activities

The Leisure Activities - a couple's satisfaction with the amount and quality of leisure time spent together.

Let your wife be a fountain of blessing for you. Rejoice in the wife of your youth. – Proverbs 5:18

Leisure Activities – Dating

We have been dating every week for 50 years. If you want to keep your relationship alive and growing, our best advice is to date your mate! Dating will help you maintain a friendship—one of the best indicators of a successful, long-term marriage. The habit of dating is the catalyst for building your couple friendship and staying emotionally connected through the coming years. This exercise will help you establish, reestablish, or reinforce the dating habit.

1. Separately write down your answers to the following questions.
   - As you think about the life of your relationship, what have been your most favorite dates?
   - What do you enjoy doing together? (sports, hobbies, interests, and recreational activities)
   - What are some things you would like to learn or pursue together? (e.g. sports, cooking, hiking)

2. Share your answers with each other and brainstorm a combined list of potential dates.

_____

_____

_____

_____

_____

_____

_____

Leisure Activities Ideas

It's easy to get stuck in a rut and do the same things over and over, we recommend that you try something new in your relationship. Review this lest and circle something you would like to try, share with your partner. Agree on 1-2 activities that you will both try together.

Acting	Concerts
Amusement Parks	Croquet
Antique Collecting	Dancing
Archery	Dinning Out
Auto Racing	Fishing
Badminton	Football (watching)
Basketball (playing)	Football (playing)
Basketball (watching)	Gardening
Bible Study	Dancing (ballroom)
Bicycling	Dancing (square)
Boating	Dancing (rock)
Bowling	Flying (as pilot)
Bridge	Flying (as passenger)
Camping	Football (watching)
Canoeing	Football (playing)
Chess	
Computer Games	

Gardening
Genealogical Golf
Ham Radio
Handball
Hiking

Hockey (watching)
Hockey (playing)
Horseback Riding
Horse Shows
(watching)
Horseracing
Horseshoe Pitching
Hot Air Ballooning
Hunting
Ice Skating
Ice Fishing
Jogging
Judo
Karate
Knitting
Metalwork
Model Building
Monopoly
Mountain Climbing
Movies
Museums

Opera
Painting
Photography
Pinochle
Play Golf

Handball
Hiking
Hockey (watching)
Poker
Polo (watching) Pool
(or billiards) Quilting
Racquetball
Remodeling (home)
Roller Skating Rock
Collecting Rowing
Rummy
Sailing
Sculpting
Shooting (skeet, trap)
Shooting (pistol)
Shopping (clothes)
Shopping (groceries)
Shopping (vehicles)
Shu ! eboard
Hockey (playing)
Horseback riding

Singing

Surfing

Skiing (water)
Skiing (downhill)
Skiing (cross country)
Skin Diving
Skydiving
Snowmobile
Softball (watching)
Softball (playing)
Spear Fishing
Stamp Collecting

Swimming
Table Tennis
Taxidermy
Television
Tennis
Toboggining
Video Production
Video Movies
Volleyball

What Does God's Word Say?

Ecclesiastes 4: 8-12

Ecclesiastes 9:9

Deuteronomy 24:5

Willard F. Harley Jr, (2002). His Needs Her Needs pages 208-213.

Leisure Activity Action Steps

- Examples of Goals:
  - Take Salsa dancing lessons
  - Go hiking together
  - Horseback riding

Goals

_____ completion date _

_____ completion date _

_____ completion date _

Sexual Relations

We continue to enjoy sex even in our old age! God designed husbands and wives for intimacy even into their old age. It is supposed to get better and better, that's God way! Our culture tells us 'Sex is good the first year," "sex gets old, we are lucky if we are intimate once a month!" Let's look at our intimacy in God's way.

Give honor to marriage, and remain faithful to one another in marriage... — Hebrews 13:4

THE EXPRESSION OF INTIMACY

Give honor to marriage, and remain faithful to one another in marriage... — Hebrews 13:4

Emotional intimacy and physical intimacy are closely related. Couples who have a good emotional relationship and feel loved and appreciated have the best physical relationship.

Affection is, to a large degree, a learned skill. Even those who seem to be "naturals" in this area usually had some training in their childhood as they saw and experienced the expressions of affection modeled around them. Those for whom affection seems awkward may have come from a home where affection was absent or rarely expressed. Either way, it's important to discuss your upbringing and how it has affected your expectations in this area.

COUPLE DISCUSSION

The following questions were designed using the definition of affection as "any verbal or nonverbal expression that communicates love in a non-sexual way."

- What does "affection" mean to you?
- How much affection was there in your families growing up (verbal and nonverbal)?
- How did you respond to the affection (or lack of affection) you received?
- How did your father show affection?
- How did your mother show affection?
- On a scale of 1-10, how much affection do you want in your marriage? (1—very little, 10—great amount)
- What do you need in order to be in the mood for sex?
- Do you feel comfortable initiating sex? Why or why not?
- How often would you prefer or expect sex?
- What sexual activities do you enjoy most?
- Are there specific sexual acts that make you uncomfortable?
- How could you each contribute to making your sexual relationship more satisfying?

Listen to your partner and take notes, then discuss.

Prepare Enrich Workbook for Couples (2014) page 27.

Mark and Karen Stevens

What Does God Word Say About Sexuality?

Proverbs 5:18-19

1 Corinthians 7:3-5

Hebrews 13:4

Ephesians 5:28

Song of Solomon 7:10-12

I Corinthians 6:19-20

Philippians 2:3-4

Intimacy Action Steps

- Examples of Goals:
  - Set a time for intimacy
  - ! Share what intimacy means to you
  - Share what you like and don't like

Goals

_____ completion date _

_____ completion date _

_____ completion date _

Roles and Responsibilities

Today we see more and more confusion and conflict about roles and responsibilities inthe home.

Make every effort to keep yourselves united in the Spirit, binding yourselves together with peace. — Ephesians 4:3

RELATIONSHIP ROLES

SHARING ROLES

List your responsibilities and your partner's responsibilities related to the household and/or children. Your partner should also separately create the same two lists.

Things You Do for your Household

_____

_____

_____

_____

_____

Things Your Partner Does for your Household

_____

_____

_____

_____

_____

_____

COUPLE DISCUSSION

- After you have each completed your lists, compare and discuss them. Any surprises?
- Are roles mainly divided by interests and skill, or by more traditional male/female roles?
- Consider for a moment how similar or dissimilar these lists are compared to what you witnessed in your parents' roles growing up.
- Discuss what each of you would like to adjust in your lists of roles. If needed, agree on how you might revise your current lists.
- Revise your current lists, finalizing an agreement about tasks you will each do in the future. Set a time to review the new lists.

SWITCHING ROLES EXERCISE

After you have each completed your Household Tasks lists, plan a day (or a week) when you can perform each other's household responsibilities. This Role Reversal experiment will help you gain a new appreciation for one another.

What Does God's Word Say?

Daily Roles and Responsibilities

I Timothy 5:8

I Thessalonians 4:10-12

11 Thessalonians 3:10-12

I Corinthians 10:31

Colossians 3:23-24

Proverbs 18:9

Godly Roles – Husband and Wife

Ephesians 5:21, 25, 29-33

Genesis 2:18

Proverbs 13:10-12, 30-31

Philillians 2:1-8

Matthew 20:28

Mark 10:45

Roles and Responsibly Action Steps

Write a list of roles and responsibilities that you both agree on:

His   Her

Spiritual Beliefs

Many couples come into their marriage with a set of spiritual beliefs. Many times, we find that they haven't really discussed what they believe and how what they believe will be lived out in their marriage.

And you must love the Lord your God with all your heart, all your soul, all your mind, and all your strength.' The second is equally important: 'Love your neighbor as yourself.' No other commandment is greater than these." — Mark 12:30-31

YOUR SPIRITUAL JOURNEY

Spirituality and faith are powerful dimensions of the human experience. Spiritual beliefs can provide a foundation for the values and behaviors of individuals and couples. People who profess a spiritual faith do, indeed, feel their beliefs breathe life into their relationships. Couples with high agreement on spiritual beliefs report much higher levels of marital satisfaction and closeness than those with low spiritual agreement.

Given the potential benefits of spiritual beliefs in a relationship, it makes sense for partners to explore and evaluate their compatibility regarding spiritual beliefs. Couples with strong spiritual beliefs and practices say their faith provides a foundation that deepens their love and helps them grow together and achieve their dreams. If you and your partner's spiritual beliefs are incompatible, talking about the origins of your beliefs can help you understand one another.

COUPLE DISCUSSION

Set aside some time to discuss the following questions together and share your individual responses. (If you do not have the answers, ask other family members about their perspective.)

- What is your family's religious tradition and heritage? How was spiritually discussed when you were a child?
- What holidays (holy days) and rituals does your family observe?
- How similar or dissimilar are your personal religious and spiritual beliefs compared to those of your family?
- What holidays (holy days) and rituals do you find personally meaningful?
- How does your spiritual life affect your values and the decisions you make?
- To what extent do you/would you like to integrate your faith or spiritual life into your marriage relationship?
- Do you have strong feelings or opinions about the spiritual upbringing you'd like to provide for your children?

- Are we in agreement for our home church and are we committed to that church?
- How has your understanding of God changed through your life and up till now?
! What activities do you and your partner do together to strengthen your spiritual walk?

Take notes as you listen to your partner:

WHAT THE BIBLE SAYS ABOUT SPIRITUAL BELIEFS

Matthew 6:33

Psalms 37:4

Proverbs 3:5-6

II Corinthians 6:14

Ephesians 6:4

Deuteronomy 6:7

Spirituality Action Steps

- Examples of Goals:
    - ! Set a time to discuss your current spiritual status
    - • Share your spiritual goals
    - ! Commit to a church home and support through giving

Goals

_____ completion date _

_____ completion date _

_____ completion date _

Action Steps

You've heard it said, "the definition of insanity is doing the same thing over and over and expecting different results!" Karen and I are all about taking actions to change our behavior and stop doing the "same things over and over!" We find that couples leave marriage seminars/retreat feeling good but not really putting into practice what they have learned. They fall back into the same old habits.

So, take action and create a habit. We want you to go back through your top areas of needed growth and pick 3 goals that you are going to put into practice. Remember it takes about 30 days to make an action a habit!

Make sure you use SMART goals = **S**pecific. **M**easurable. **A**chievable. **R**ealistic and **T**imebound.

Examples of a Smart Goal: We will have a date night every Friday night from 7PM-9PM. We will pray together every night at 9PM.

Goals

1._____
   Start Date:_____
   X-times: (per day, week, month)_____
   Time:_____Day:_____

2._____
   Start Date:_____
   X-times: (per day, week, month)_____
   Time:_____Day:_____

3._____
   Start Date:_____
   X-times: (per day, week, month)_____
   Time:_____Day:_____

Recommended Resources

The Couple Check-up Book – David Olson

Prepare Enrich Workbook for Couples

Love and Respect – Emerson Eggerich

Helping Marriages - Parrott

Marriage in the Whirlwind – Farrell & Farrell

His Needs Her Needs – Willard Harley

Have a New Sex Life by Friday – Dr. Kevin Leman

Men are like Waffles and Women are Like Spaghetti – Bill and Pam Farrell

www.marriageRefuge.com for The Couple Check-up coaching and weekend retreats with Mark and Karen Stevens

Made in the USA
Monee, IL
28 June 2022